Siu Lim Tau (Little Idea)

Siu Lim Tau

For the

Solo Student

Written by

Mark Beardsell

Copyright Mark Beardsell 2010

Siu Lim Tau (Little Idea)

Index

Dedication	Page 4
Preface	Page 5
What is Wing Chun	Page 6
Chapter 1 – About the Author	Page 7
Ip Man Code of Conduct	Page 11
Chapter 2 - History	Page 13
Chapter 3 – Siu Lim Tau (Section 1)	Page 16
Opening the Stance	Page 16
The centreline, vertical midline and Six gates	Page 19
Character Sun thrusting punch	Page 21
Tan sau (left side)	Page 23
Sam bai fut (left side)	Page 24
Pak sau (left side)	Page 17
Ching cheung (left side)	Page 28
Tan sau (right side)	Page 29
Sam bai fut (right side)	Page 30
Pak sau (right side)	Page 32
Ching cheung (right side)	Page 33
Chapter 4– Siu Lim Tau (Section 2)	Page 35
Gum sau (all directions)	Page 35
Lan sau	Page 38
Fak sau	Page 39
Lan sau	Page 40
Jum sau	Page 41
Jut sau	Page 42
Biu jee sau	Page 43
Long bridge down	Page 44
Long bridge up	Page 44
Chapter 5 – Siu Lim Tau (Section 3)	Page 46
Pak sau (left side)	Page 46

Siu Lim Tau (Little Idea)

Index Continued...

Jum cheung (left side)	Page 47
Pak sau (right side)	Page 48
Jum cheung (right side)	Page 49
Tan sau (left side)	Page 50
Guan sau (left side)	Page 50
Tan sau (left side)	Page 51
Tan sau (right side)	Page 52
Guan sau (right side)	Page 53
Tan sau (right side)	Page 54
Bong sau (left side)	Page 55
Tan sau (left side)	Page 56
Dai cheung (left side)	Page 56
Bong sau (right side)	Page 56
Tan sau (right side)	Page 57
Dai cheung (right side)	Page 57
Tut sau	Page 57
Lin wan kuen	Page 59
Chapter 6 - Using the techniques	Page 64
Punching (Lin wan kuen)	Page 64
Turning	Page 65
Turning Punch	Page 66
Stepping	Page 66
Gum sau bear hug escape	Page 68
Setting up bong sau	Page 68
Jum sau	Page 69
Long bridge up and down	Page 70
Don chi sau	Page 71
Don chi sau as partner 1	Page 71
Don chi sau as partner 2	Page 72
Ching sun gerk	Page 73
Chapter 7 – The full Siu Lim Tau	Page 74

Siu Lim Tau (Little Idea)

Dedication

This book is dedicated to all those past and present who have guided me on my Wing Chun journey and without whose knowledge, guidance and patience it would not be possible to pass on this gift to help those on similar paths achieve their goals, this book is my way of thanking you all.

A big thanks to my father for is thirst for knowledge of martial arts and dragging me to classes which without I would not have been able to write this book.

I would also like to thank my Sifu Grandmaster Samuel Kwok for taking me under his wing and for passing on the Wing Chun of Ip Man in accordance with his wishes so that it will not be forgotten, which I, in turn will pass onto as many people as I can.

Siu Lim Tau (Little Idea)

Preface

The Siu Lim Tau is seldom understood by the potential student and many think they are beyond the beginning and here lies their first mistake, they want to train very quickly and move up to the intermediate Chum Kiu and the Advanced Biu Jee and everyone wants to get a Muk Yan Chong and get straight into it, myself included!.

Its not till much later in your training that you understand why Wing Chun is progressive, the Siu Lim Tau teaches you the correct posture and structure for each hand position, the footwork while looking very goofy its there to make your legs strong for things to come such as the Chum Kiu and so on. So with your leg strength and correct hand position and an understanding of what each hand position is for you can then move on to the next level which would by Chum Kiu, in this book we are going to focus on purely the Siu Lim Tau.

This book is intended for the Student who is having trouble finding a school or a training partner or even a Teacher, while this book will help you grasp the basic movements it is strongly recommended that you do find a teacher to help you with the finer points that as a beginner you will not be aware of.

Siu Lim Tau (Little Idea)

What is Wing Chun?

The short answer is Chinese Kung Fu, Wing Chun is different to the other styles of kung fu that you have seen where moves are very flamboyant with high flying kicks and stunning acrobatics, Wing Chun is for close quarter combat, it's very quick, very direct, and with economy of movement a lot of power is released in it's strikes making it an awesome martial art to learn.

The western world only started to see Wing Chun way back in the late 1960's and early 1970's when Bruce Lee came on the big screen this is when we were first introduced to Wing Chun, and the first schools that Bruce Lee opened up in the USA were Wing Chun schools, he later went on to develop his Jeet Kune Do – The way of the intercepting fist, Bruce lee was taught Wing Chun by Ip Man before he moved to the USA, and so the interest in Wing Chun started to grow.

Siu Lim Tau (Little Idea)

Chapter 1 - About the Author

My marital arts journey started way back in 1971 at the age of 7 when my Father had the job of baby sitting BUT had an Aikido class to teach at the same, so off we went to Thornaby pavilion, what better way to keep an eye on the kids and teach a class, I am sure at that time my Father never even thought that I would get hooked on the subject.

So from the age of seven I began learning Aikido, there was always a selection of Judo, Aikido and Karate books lying around the house that I would always pick up and have a read and try out various techniques, I never did really learn the whole Aikido system, but learned enough about the subject to kick arse at school and can only remember coming close to getting beat a couple of times, Aikido gave me an edge. Around the age of eighteen I went off to learn Karate under a guy called Bernard Creton at Folkestone sport centre, he was teaching his own style at the time called Jutsu Kai, i only lasted about 6 months at the class and I never graded but was told I was ready for my blue belt, I continued to practice the kicks at home and at my Father's Aikido dojo as having one hand I thought the kicks would give me an advantage, I still practice those kicks today, thanks Hanshi Bernard Creton 8th Dan, the following year, lead by my Father, we started attending a Judo school, there was a

Siu Lim Tau (Little Idea)

class around the corner and one in the next town of Hawkinge on a Sunday so I spent sometime doing this and gained a yellow belt.

I never did much of anything else over the next 20 years, but kept my skills going, and then I decided to examine my martial arts roots, which led me to my Father's Aikido teacher in Malaysia who taught him in 1958, Sensei Thamby Rajah 10th Dan, I learned he was still alive and both me and my Father took a trip over to Malaysia and spent two weeks there learning Aikido with the masters and Thamby Rajah Sensei at a Gasshuku in 2006, also making a number of friends along the way. By this time I had also started studying Wing Chun and had been for around a year.

Siu Lim Tau (Little Idea)

There were no Wing Chun schools where I live so I turned to the internet, and tried a few distance learning courses but they did not really amount to anything, I really wanted to grow and get it right then I took a chance on Sifu Phil Bradley's distance learning course and just got better and better, his course really does work, but of course I could not do any chi sau as I was the only person in my area doing Wing Chun. So with his support and at this time completing the course to the level of Siu Nim Tau I opened my doors to students to give me a chance to make my Wing Chun better.

AWCA 2008 summer camp in Phoenix, Arizona

While with the Arizona Wing Chun Association, I attended their training events in Chicago, Arizona and North Carolina, and in late 2008 being with the AWCA for 2 years I wanted to learn the dummy form but the AWCA have a strict progressive policy so I looked towards more traditional styles and found that Sifu Sam Chan in Michigan, he had a certification program so after re-certifying my

Siu Lim Tau (Little Idea)

Siu Lim Tau and Chum Kiu I set about learning his dummy form, then, in April of 2009 while attending a 10 day training camp with Grandmaster Samuel Kwok, I decided to follow his example and pass on Ip Man Traditional Wing Chun, and in August 2009 I became a formal student of Grandmaster Samuel Kwok and my journey begins. As a disciple I was given a name that best suits me and that name was Kwok Chung Yin, Yin means good to/with people.

Picture above is from April 2009 summer camp in Portugal

Lineages

1. Ip Man ⇨ Leung Ting ⇨ Robert Jaquet ⇨ Don Grose ⇨ Phil Bradley ⇨ Me

2. Ip Man ⇨ Ip Ching ⇨ Sam Hing Fai Chan ⇨ Me

3. Ip Man ⇨ Ip Chun/Ip Ching ⇨ Samuel Kwok ⇨ Me

Anyone studying Wing Chun from me will be taught the third lineage.

Siu Lim Tau (Little Idea)

Ip Man Code of Conduct

守 紀 律 崇 尚 武 德

Remain disciplined - uphold yourself ethically as a martial artist

明 禮 義 愛 國 尊 親

Practice courtesy and righteousness - serve the community and honour your family

愛 同 學 團 結 樂 群

Love your fellow students or classmates - be united and avoid conflicts

節 色 慾 保 守 精 神

Limit your desires and pursuit of bodily pleasures - preserve the proper spirit

勤 練 習 技 不 離 身

Train diligently and make it a habit - maintain your skills

學 養 氣 救 濫 鬥 民

Learn to develop spiritual tranquillity - abstain from arguments and fights

Siu Lim Tau (Little Idea)

民 溫 度 態 世 處 常

Participate in society - be conservative, cultured and gentle in your manners

仁 輔 武 以 小 弱 扶

Help the weak and the very young - use your martial skill for the good of humanity

訓 祖 持 漢 緒 光 繼

Pass on the tradition - preserve this Chinese art and its rules of conduct

Siu Lim Tau (Little Idea)

Chapter 2 – History

I tell you the history of Wing Chun, because it is important that you know the source of the water that you drink from. Are the words Ip Man used often I am told.

In the late 1600's and early 1700's Kung Fu became very popular at the Siu Lam (Shaolin) monastery in Honan Province, Siu Lam or Shaolin translates to " little trees", The Kung Fu exercises were designed to help keep the monks and abbots awake during long periods of mental training and meditation. By exercising their bodies as well as their minds they developed even further in their spiritual training. The Manchu (non-Chinese) government in the North at the time were deeply suspicious of such activities, believing the monastery to be training an army. They eventually attacked the monastery, burning it to the ground and killing many of the monks and disciples. A few escaped the attack though, and they are thought to have been the Buddhist nun Ng Mui, Abbot Chi Shin, Abbot Pak Mei, Fung To Tak and Master Miu Hin.

So Wing Chun was first heard of around 300 to 400 years ago when the Shaolin nun who had escaped the temple, first introduced this style to a young woman, the daughter of a bean curd trader by the name of Yim Yee, she was being perused by a suitor who wanted to marry her, but she was not interested, and was trying to dissuade him. Ng Mui seeing her plight approached her and offered to teach her this new style to defend herself against the suitor, this style worked well because of a woman's physical frame being smaller than that of a man and worked well for fighting and also the pigeon toed footwork suited the bound feet of the Chinese women of the time too.

Siu Lim Tau (Little Idea)

Like all kung fu styles, this style was based on the movements of animals in this case the snake and crane. It is said that Ng Mui spent many hours observing the movements of these creatures leading up to developing this new style of kung fu.

The original snake and crane style had only the Siu Lim Tau and the Bart Cham Dao as that was all that was needed at that time. Needless to say that Yim Wing Chun went on to beat the suitor and he left here alone after that. Yim Wing Chun sometime in the future went on to marry a man by the name of Leung Bok Chau who was an accomplished martial artist, but on seeing this new style that was taught to his wife, asked her to teach him, this she did and later on her husband named the style Wing Chun after his wife.

Leung Bok Chau went on to pass Wing Chun on to a man by the name of Leung Lan Kwai, who in turn passed it on to Wong Wah Bo then to Leung Yee Tai, it was at this time that Leung Yee Tai met Abbot Chi Shin hiding away as a cook with the Red opera and Chi Shin taught the pole to Leung Yee Tai, some time later Leung Yee Tai met Wong Wah Bo who passed Wing Chun on to Leung Yee Tai in exchange for teaching him the pole, and so the Lik dim boon kwan (*six and a half point long pole*) was added to the system.

It was at this time that Leung Yee Tai passed Wing Chun on to a young man by the name of Leung Jan, he is known for adding clarity and definition to the Wing Chun system, by that I mean he became the most accomplished student of Wing Chun and went about writing down the system for future students to learn from. It's about this time that we become aware of the addition of the Mok Yan Jong (Wooden Man) the Chum Kiu form (bridge seeking/sinking) and the emergency techniques for the advanced student know as the Biu Jee. Leung Jan went on to teach many his system but most notably was Chan Wah Shun and his elder son

Siu Lim Tau (Little Idea)

Leung Bik. This is where things really start to get familiar, Wing Chun was then taught to many in Foshan/Fatsan but the one name that is popular around the world today is IP Man aka Yip Man, a name made famous by the exploits of our all time favourite Bruce Lee, we saw our first Wing Chun taught to Non-Chinese in America.

Ip Man first learned Wing Chun under Chan Wah Shun also know as Chan the money changer as that was his profession, Chan Wah Shun died before completing Ip Man's Wing Chun training and so his training was finished by his Si-hing, after the Japanese invasion of China, Ip Man escaped to Hong Kong and began openly teaching Wing Chun there, it was here that he met Leung Jan's son Leung Bik, it is said that the young, very sure of himself Ip man could not be beaten and when given the chance to fight with this man, IP man was beaten by him and went away a little disgruntled, later he was to learn on a second encounter with this man that he was Leung Bik, and with that IP Man became his student, Chan Wah Shun was quite a bulky person so his Wing Chun came across very heavy, however the Wing Chun of Leung Bik was soft and this is what allowed Leung Bik to overcome Ip Man. Sadly Ip Man passed away in 1972 but his two sons Ip Chun and Ip Ching continue to pass Wing Chun around the world most notably today is Samuel Kwok who works very hard in promoting Wing Chun world wide.

Siu Lim Tau (Little Idea)

Chapter 3 – Siu Lim Tau (Section 1)

Opening the stance

The Siu Lim Tau starts from a straight stood up position like standing to attention with your arms by your sides and looking forward.

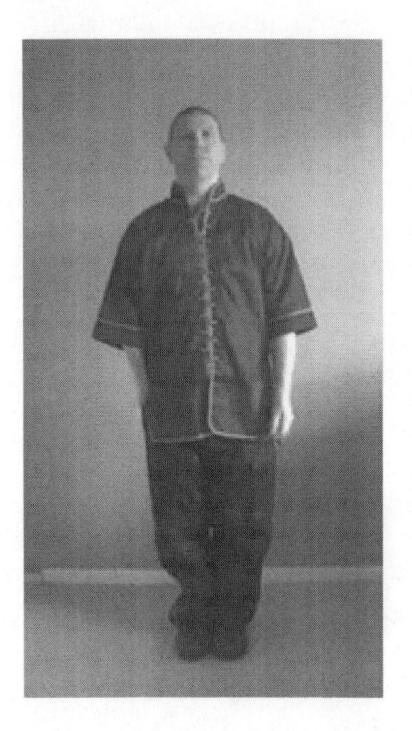

The first thing we learn is called "opening the stance" the Chinese for this is Hoi ma

Bring your forearms up horizontal with your body at the same time your elbows are travelling behind you as if you were striking

Siu Lim Tau (Little Idea)

somebody behind you with them, I'll go on to call this chambering. Bend your knees just enough so that you can see your toes just over the end of your knees, but don't get in the habit of looking down all the time to check this it does not have to be perfect its just a guideline.

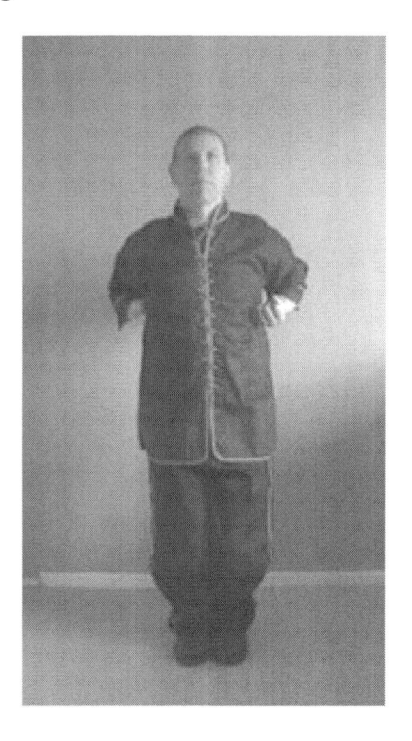

During this step, the gap between the ground and the sole of your foot should be only a small gap.

Keeping your heels on the ground move the toes on each foot outwardly until a 90 degree angle is achieved; note your left foot would be pointing out 45 degrees in the left direction and right foot, 45 degrees in the right direction.

Siu Lim Tau (Little Idea)

Now switch the weight to your toes, pushing your heels outwardly until you can visualise a triangle on the ground made up at the base with your feet travelling off towards a point in front of you about 1 metre. Your feet should be roughly at an angle of 60 degrees.

You have now opened the stance, once you have completed hoi-ma and you are stationary, this position is now called yee gee kim yeung ma which translates to character two stance. The Chinese character for two is made up of two horizontal lines the lower line is wider than the upper line thus explaining the position of your feet.

Siu Lim Tau (Little Idea)

The centreline, vertical midline and Six gates.

While stood in yee gee kim yeung ma send your fingers down outwardly and crossing at the wrists left on top of right, your arms should be fully locked out and if you check the distance of your elbows they should be one fist distance from the body, this position is know as double gaun sau or gow cha gaun sau.

Then imagine there is a vertical pole in front of you and your crossed hands are currently touching the pole in the lower position this line is called the vertical midline, bring your hands straight upwards along the route of that invisible pole and stop when your hands reaches a point just above your solar plexus, this position is called double tan sau or gow cha tan sau, if you draw a line horizontally from one nipple to the other then the point in the middle that meets the vertical midline is your centreline you should stop at this point, your hands should still be crossed and about 7 inches away, one open hand in front of your solar plexus.

Siu Lim Tau (Little Idea)

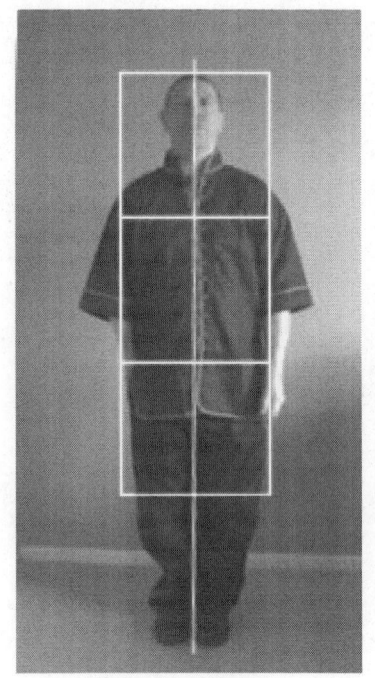

The six gates

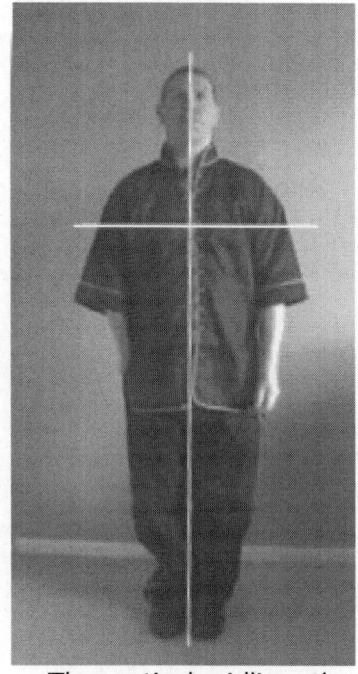

The vertical midline, the centre of cross is the centreline.

Huh? What's all that about I here you say, and you will not be the first person to ask that question I think every Wing Chun student has asked that question, well there are several schools of thought, I'll let you make your own mind up, the most common is that these first movements instil in your mind guan sau and tan sau and training both hands at the same time for speed. Another theory and the one I have described in this book is that the movements are there to remind us of where our vertical midline is, where our

Siu Lim Tau (Little Idea)

centreline is located and to remind us of the six gates that we use to attack and defend are found.

To finish off this set, as we did at the start, bring your forearms up horizontal with your body at the same time your elbows are travelling behind you as if you were striking somebody behind you with them. This is sometimes referred to as the chambered position.

Character sun thrusting punch

Welcome to your first strike, to put it simple Wing Chun is a fist fighting martial art and some times you will here it referred to as Wing Chun Kuen, which translates to eternal springtime fist, it is called the character sun thrusting punch because if you look at your fist with your thumb to the top and your little finger to the bottom and your fist is in vertical position then your fist looks like the Chinese character for the word sun.

Returning to the position I left you in yee gee kim yeung ma, bring your left fist to your centreline, as your fist travels out to the centreline it should travel out diagonally in a straight line to a point on the centreline which is one hand open distance from the body... pause for a second and imagine a straight line away from you through the centreline... then using your elbow drive your fist out along that invisible line and stop at full extension of the arm. Keep your arm locked out and open your hand with your palm facing up. Slowly lift your fingers as to beckon somebody to you, then rotate the wrist clockwise until your fingers are pointing down and then

Siu Lim Tau (Little Idea)

close your hand to make a fist... pause... and then retract the arm to the position you first started at.

Repeating this on the right side bring your right fist to your centreline, as your fist travels out to the centreline it should travel out diagonally in a straight line to a point on the centreline which is one hand open distance from the body... pause for a second and imagine a straight line away from you through the centreline... then using your elbow drive your fist out along that invisible line and stop at full extension of the arm. Keep your arm locked out and open your hand with your palm facing up. Slowly lift your fingers as to beckon somebody to you, then rotate the wrist anti-clockwise until your fingers are pointing down and then close your hand to make a fist... pause... and then retract the arm to the position you first started at.

Siu Lim Tau (Little Idea)

Tan sau (Left Side**)**

The next movement in the Siu Lim Tau is called tan sau sometimes called beggar hand or simply know as palm up hand, enacting this movements involves keeping your elbow pointed to the ground, and a bend at the elbow so your arm makes up two sides of a triangle, your wrist should also be bent with you palm facing upwards, and your elbow should be one fist distance from your body and the inside of your forearm should just be to the side of your centreline.

To start off take up the yee gee kim yeung ma position and bring your forearms up horizontal with your body at the same time your elbows are travelling behind you as if you were striking somebody behind you with them or pulling them towards you.

Open your left hand and imagine a magnet is holding your little finger against your torso and slowly move your hand forward which will travel along your torso because its magnetically held there, when your middle finger finally reaches your centreline then imagine someone is puling your finger away from your and outwardly through your centreline, keep the whole hand with the palm up travelling out until your elbow is one fist distance from the body and hold there.

Siu Lim Tau (Little Idea)

Sam Bai Fut (Left Side)

Wing Chun terminology if you did not know is in Cantonese so sam bai fut translates as three prays to Buddha, if something is considered important in Wing Chun and the ancestors wanted you to realise that there is more to the technique than meets the eye then they repeat it three times in the forms as a signal to pay attention to this, your first introduction to this is sam bai fut. There are three movements in this cycle; these are called wu sau, heun sau and fook sau.

So, returning to the last position you were in... remember I said hold it there, just to recap you are currently in yee gee kim yeung ma, your right hand is retracted and your left hand is in tan sau.

Slowly lift your fingers as to beckon somebody to you, then rotate the wrist clockwise until your fingers are pointing down then throw

Siu Lim Tau (Little Idea)

your fingers away from you and allow them to travel upwards 180 degrees, your fingers/hand should now be in the praying position the transition from tan sau to wu sau was called heun sau leading to jut sau, the position you are now in is referred to as wu sau.

Keeping your elbow still and your hand in wu sau allow the wrist to travel backwards towards your body, and keep that wrist on the centreline too, keep travelling backwards until you reach a minimum of one fist distance from the body, now allow your hand to relax and

Siu Lim Tau (Little Idea)

your fingers to fall loose, your hand should now be horizontal and your fingers pointing to the right, slowly move your hand directly outwards, away from you, the wrist should be kept on the centreline, keep going out until the elbow clears the body and there is a gap between your elbow and your torso of one fist.

This time from your current hand position rotate the wrist clockwise until your fingers are pointing down then throw your fingers away from you and allow them to travel upwards 180 degrees on completion you will find your hand is again in wu sau.

Again keeping your elbow still and your hand in wu sau allow the wrist to travel backwards towards your body, and keep that wrist on the centreline, keep travelling backwards until you reach a minimum of one fist distance from the body, now allow your hand to relax and your fingers to fall loose, your hand should now be horizontal and your fingers pointing to the right, slowly move your hand directly outwards, away from you, the wrist should be kept on the centreline, keep going outward until the elbow clears the body and there is a gap between your elbow and torso of one fist.

Again from your current hand position rotate the wrist clockwise until your fingers are pointing down, then throw your fingers away from you and allow them to travel upwards 180 degrees on completion you will find your hand is again in wu sau.

And for the third time keeping your elbow still and your hand in wu sau allow the wrist to travel backwards towards your body, and keep that wrist on the centreline, keep travelling backwards until you reach a minimum distance of one fist from the body, allow your hand to relax and your finger to fall loose, your hand should now be horizontal and your fingers pointing to the right, slowly move your hand directly outwards, away from you, the wrist should be kept on

Siu Lim Tau (Little Idea)

the centreline, keep going out until the elbow clears the body and there is a gap between your elbow and your torso of one fist.

This will complete the third wu sau hence the Cantonese phrase sam bai fut which takes us to the next movement of pak sau.

Pak sau (Left Side)

This hand movement looks similar to wu sau, the action of pak sau is to push away an obstacle that has entered your centreline space as this pak sau is on the left hand we our pushing the obstacle away from left to right, the palm is doing the pushing, when the palm reaches the right shoulder seam stop, pak sau never travels beyond this point.

So as we are currently stood in yee gee kim yeung ma with your right hand retracted and your left hand in wu sau which is on the

Siu Lim Tau (Little Idea)

centreline and at least one fist distance from the body, move your left hand from left to right and stop at the shoulder seam, now reverse your hand along the path it travelled outward putting you back in the wu sau position and pause.

Ching cheung (Left Side)

The word for palm strike on Cantonese is cheung and the word for forward is ching or jing, so this is a forward palm strike.

Keep your wrist in the same place and your fingers pointing up, move the blade of your hand to the left thus forcing your palm to face away from you, now shoot your palm forward in a straight line just as you did with the punch.

And just like the punch keep your arm locked out rotate your wrist through 180 degrees so that your palm is now face up. Slowly lift

Siu Lim Tau (Little Idea)

your finger as to beckon somebody to you, then rotate the wrist clockwise until your fingers are pointing down and then close your hand to make a fist... pause... and then retract the arm to the chambered position you first started at.

This completes the left hand side of section one.

No we have to repeat everything on the right hand side.

Tan sau (Right Side)

From the yee gee kim yeung ma position and your arms in the chambered position.

Open your right hand and imagine a magnet is holding your little finger against your torso and slowly move your hand forward which will travel along your torso because its magnetically held there,

Siu Lim Tau (Little Idea)

when your middle finger finally reaches your centreline imagine someone is puling your finger away from you outwardly through your centreline, keep the whole hand with the palm up travelling out until your elbow is one fist distance from the body and hold there.

Sam Bai Fut (Right Side)

Slowly lift your fingers as to beckon somebody to you, then rotate the wrist anti-clockwise until your fingers are pointing down then throw your fingers away from you and allow them to travel upwards through 180 degrees, your fingers/hand should now be in the praying position, you are now in what is called wu sau.

Keeping your elbow still and your hand in wu sau allow the wrist to travel backwards towards your body, and keep that wrist on the centreline, keep travelling backwards until you reach a minimum of one fist distance from the body, now allow your hand to relax and

Siu Lim Tau (Little Idea)

your fingers to fall loose, your hand should now be horizontal and your fingers pointing to the left, slowly move your hand directly outwards, away from you, the wrist should be kept on the centreline, keep going out until the elbow clears the body and there is a gap between your elbow and your torso of one fist.

This time from your current hand position rotate the wrist anti-clockwise until your fingers are pointing down then throw your fingers away from you and allow them to travel upwards through 180 degrees on completion you will find your hand is again in wu sau.

And again keeping your elbow still and your hand in wu sau allow the wrist to travel backwards towards your body, and keep that wrist on the centreline, keep travelling backwards until you reach a minimum of one fist distance from the body, now allow your hand to relax and your fingers to fall loose, your hand should now be horizontal and your fingers pointing to the left, slowly move your hand directly outwards, away from you, the wrist should be kept on the centreline, keep going out until the elbow clears the body and there is a gap between your elbow and torso of one fist.

Again from your current hand position rotate the wrist anti-clockwise until your fingers are pointing down, then throw your fingers away from you and allow them to travel upwards through 180 degrees on completion you will find your hand is again in wu sau

One more time, keeping your elbow still and your hand in wu sau allow the wrist to travel backwards towards your body, and keep that wrist on the centreline, keep travelling backwards until you reach a minimum of one fist distance from the body, now allow your hand to relax and your fingers to fall loose, your hand should now be horizontal and your fingers pointing to the left, then slowly move

Siu Lim Tau (Little Idea)

your hand directly outwards, away from you, the wrist should be kept on the centreline, keep going out until the elbow clears the body and there is a gap between your elbow and your torso of one fist.

Pak sau (Right Side)

Move your right hand from right to left and stop at the shoulder seam. Now reverse your hand along the path it travelled outward putting you back in the wu sau position and pause.

Siu Lim Tau (Little Idea)

Ching cheung (Right Side)

Keep your wrist in the same place and your fingers pointing up move the blade of your hand to the right thus forcing your palm outward; now shoot your palm forward in a straight line just as you did with the punch.

And just like the punch keep your arm locked out and open your hand with your palm facing up. Slowly lift your fingers as to beckon somebody to you, then rotate the wrist anti-clockwise until your fingers are pointing down and then close your hand to make a fist... pause... and then retract the arm to the position you first started at.

Siu Lim Tau (Little Idea)

This completes section one of the Siu Lim tau, I really recommend practicing this for at least three months before moving onto to section 2, it's a good idea to spread out each section over a three month period and train a couple of times a week for around 1 hour to really get good at it.

Siu Lim Tau (Little Idea)

Chapter 4– Siu Lim Tau (Section 2)

In section two of the Siu Lim Tau you will find that most of it, is performed with both hands at the same time barring gum sau to the side, at the beginning of the section, in Siu Lim Tau section one the focus was on teaching you good hand positions and how to build the energy required for each technique, section two of the Siu Lim Tau however teaches you how to release that energy.

Gum sau (all directions)

Section two of the Siu Lim tau starts off with gum sau to the side, we always start with the left side there are many explanations to why we start on the left hand side but my favourite theory is that most people are right handed so they will lead an attack such as a punch with the right hand, if we train to use the left hand first we become like the south paw and we are able to meet the attack quicker than having to cross arms, right arm for right arm and most people do not expect to be attacked with the left hand first, sneaky huh!.

So back to gum sau, gum sau is also known as downwards pak sau, the palm of the hand faces the floor and from the moment that hand is opened it shoots down, the contact point is the heal of the hand, there is no pause, and on completion the hand should be flat and the arms should be at full extension, also the hand should finish a few inches away from the body.

So starting from your yee gee kim yeung ma and your hand withdrawn in the ready position enact gum sau on the left and side pause... then do the right hand side. Always place a small pause between each action.

Siu Lim Tau (Little Idea)

Siu Lim Tau (Little Idea)

Your hands now move from the side to the small of the back with your palms facing away from you, shoot your arms out at the same time keeping them symmetrical and as close to each other as you can, bring your hands back to the small of your back, your palms still away from you slide your hands one each side, to the front of your body so that they are next to each other and the palms are pointing away from you and down at a 45 degree angle. Again shoot them out on the direction the palms are pointing and hold.

Siu Lim Tau (Little Idea)

Lan sau

At the same time bring both forearms up with the palms flat, the right arm pointing left and the left arm pointing right, the right forearm should be under the left, and your fingertips should line up with each elbow and both forearms, one above, and one below your centreline and pause. I sometimes jokingly refer to this as the genie position.

As stated before we are only training both hands at the same time for the sake of speed, lan sau translates as bar arm so if someone is too close you can block there way by raising the arm in to the lan sau position it does not matter which arm you use.

Siu Lim Tau (Little Idea)

Fak sau

Keeping your eyes front, slice out to the left and right at the same time, remember we are training both hands at the same time so visualise striking a face or throat with the blade of the hand.

Siu Lim Tau (Little Idea)

Lan sau

At the same time bring both arms back in, this time though, the left forearm should be under the right and your finger tips should line up with each elbow of both forearms and be one above and one below your centreline and pause.

The next movement is a bit trickier...

Siu Lim Tau (Little Idea)

Jum sau

From your lan sau position, drop your elbows, this forcing your forearms up, and keeping your hands flat so that now your palms are facing each other and are a mirror of each other, drop your forearms 90 degrees forward like they are on hinges at the elbow, be mindful not to move the elbows, this sinking action is called jum sau and is used for blocking an attack that has compromised our centreline.

Siu Lim Tau (Little Idea)

Jut sau

Jut sau is very similar to jum sau as the actions are difficult to tell apart, the easiest way to remember this is that jum sau sinks and jut sau judders, so if you see what looks like jum sau and there is a jerk in the movement then it is actually jut sau.

So your forearms and hands are a mirror of each other and note that each action from here is simultaneous so move your left palm anti-clockwise and your right palm clockwise until your palms are facing upwards, pause, now turn your left palm clockwise and your right palm anti-clockwise at the same time until both palms are facing down but simultaneously jerk your elbows back about one to two inches and pause.

Siu Lim Tau (Little Idea)

Biu jee sau

"Biu" translates as to travel quickly or to dart when followed by "jee" means fingers so it could be said as darting fingers when followed by "ma" it means darting step or stance, in this case we are saying "biu jee sau" so a rough translation would be fast finger hand.

As you hear my say throughout the book, from the point where I left you paused, shoot your fingers out and up towards the eyes of an imaginary opponent of about the same height as yourself, go to full extension of the arm and keep the arms locked out and pause.

Siu Lim Tau (Little Idea)

Long bridge down (cheong kiu gum sau**)**

Keeping your arms locked out, allow your arms to travel down with your palms facing down to the ground and stop when you reach waist height, and then make a small pause.

Long bridge up (tie sau**)**

From the lower position relax your hands and fingers allowing them to drop naturally so that your fingers are pointing to the ground then add a little tension to the back of the wrist and bring your hands up quickly using the back of the wrist as the attacking weapon and stop when you reach mouth height.

Siu Lim Tau (Little Idea)

To finish make fists with your hands and withdraw the elbows to the ready/chambered position to conclude section two.

This concludes section two of the Siu Lim Tau.

Siu Lim Tau (Little Idea)

Chapter 5 – Siu Lim Tau (Section 3)

Well done making it this far, this is the start of the third part of the Siu Lim Tau, while sections one and two focused on getting your structure, position, your leg strength better and also how to use the energy correctly, this is where we learn to combine what you have learned so far.

Pak sau (left side**)**

We start this section with pak sau, you will remember pak sau from the first section at the end of the sam bai fut, and this pak sau comes directly from the chambered arm position.
So while stood in yee gee kim yeung ma and both hands are at

Siu Lim Tau (Little Idea)

chest height and are chambered, bring your left hand up and across to perform pak sau then pause.

Jum cheung (left side)

Jum cheung sometimes called gwoy cheung is a palm strike if enacted with the left hand the fingers should be pointing left.

So from your pak sau position, move your fingers 90 degrees to the left at the same time bring your wrist on to the centreline then thrust your hand out to full extension, the point of contact on your hand is the lower blade section of the hand.

Siu Lim Tau (Little Idea)

Slowly lift your fingers as to beckon somebody to you, then rotate the wrist clockwise until your fingers are pointing down and then close your hand to make a fist... pause... and then retract the arm to the position you first started from, and as just a reminder this action is called **huen sau**.

Pak sau (right side)

Again while stood in yee gee kim yeung ma and both hands are at chest height and are chambered, bring your left hand up and across to perform pak sau then pause.

Siu Lim Tau (Little Idea)

Jum cheung (right side)

As we are on the opposite hand now, move your fingers 90 degrees to the right at the same time bring your wrist on to the centreline then thrust your hand out to full extension, As explained earlier the point of contact on your hand is the lower blade section.

Slowly lift your fingers as to beckon somebody to you, then rotate the wrist anti-clockwise until your fingers are pointing down and then close your hand to make a fist... pause... and then retract the arm to the position you first started in.

Siu Lim Tau (Little Idea)

Tan sau (left side)

Ah! Your thinking I know this one we did this in section one, yes you did BUT, this one is done differently.

While being stood in yee gee kim yeung ma and both hands are at chest height and are chambered, imagine a horizontal shallow crescent moon from where your left hand is outward to your centreline, as your hand leaves your side allow the hand and wrist to travel through this shape ending up in the position that you are now familiar with which is known as tan sau, and pause.

Gaun sau (left side)

This is the first time you have encountered guan sau, this is translated from Cantonese as splitting block arm and is used for blocking low strikes such as upper cuts and also strikes from the side.

Siu Lim Tau (Little Idea)

Returning to the position I left you paused in which was tan sau, keeping your elbow still as much as possible as when we start the transition for guan sau the elbow should move as little as possible. Keeping your fingers flat, your left hand travels downwards through a 90 degree trajectory, keep going till your thumb knuckle is in the centre of your thigh BUT, not touching your thigh, your hand should be just far enough away from the side of the body to protect it as this is a block to protect you from an attack to the side. Always take a small pause between each movement

Tan sau (left side**)**

This tan sau is basically the reverse of what you just did so following the opposite trajectory return your hand to tan sau, now perform heun sau but this time allow the hand to travel around by lifting up

Siu Lim Tau (Little Idea)

your thumb knuckle and directing your fingers off to the left so that your hand can be found in the jum cheung position, thrust your hand forward to full extension then perform huen sau again and retract the arm back to the chambered position.

Tan sau (right side)

Just like the left side, while being stood in yee gee kim yeung ma and both hands are at chest height and are chambered, imagine a horizontal shallow crescent moon from where your right hand is outward to your centreline, as your hand leaves your side allow the hand and wrist to travel through this shape ending up in tan sau.

Siu Lim Tau (Little Idea)

Gaun sau (right side)

From tan sau, keeping your elbow still as much as possible as when we start the transition for guan sau the elbow should move as little as possible. Keeping your fingers flat, your right hand travels downwards through 90 degrees , keep going till your thumb knuckle is in the centre of your thigh BUT, not touching your thigh, your hand should be just far enough away from the side of the body.

Siu Lim Tau (Little Idea)

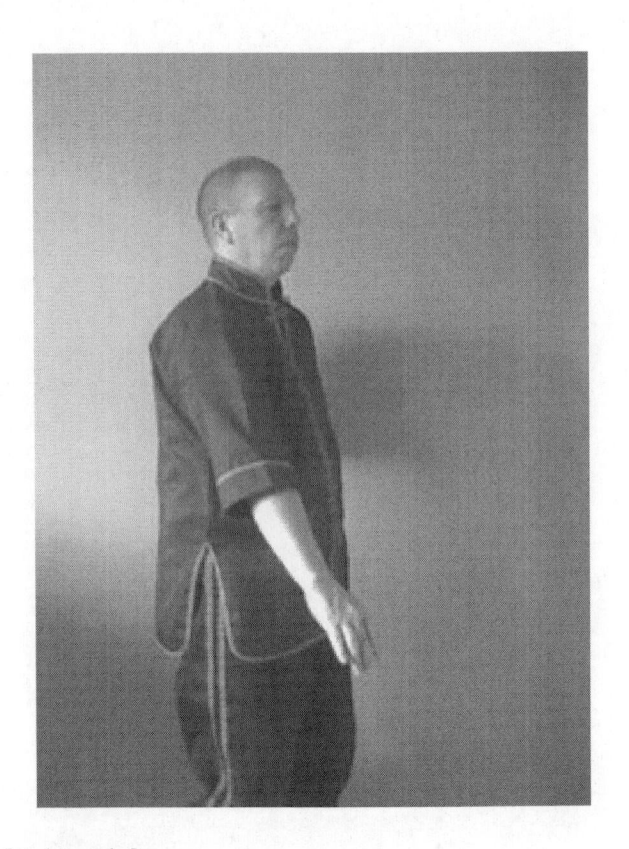

Tan sau (right side)

As enacted on the left side, this tan sau is basically the reverse of what you just did, so following the opposite trajectory return you hand to tan sau, now perform heun sau but this time allow the hand to travel around by lifting up your thumb knuckle and directing your fingers off to the right so that your hand can be found in the jum cheung position, thrust your hand forward to full extension then perform huen sau, once again retract the arm back to the chambered position.

Siu Lim Tau (Little Idea)

Bong sau (left side)

For details on how to perform a good bong sau see page 68

Assuming that you have read the bong sau section as suggested and that you are stood on yee gee kim yeung ma with your hands at chest height and your elbows are chambered in one smooth action open your left hand and bring your forearm out while turning over your hand so your little finger is on the top and your thumb is on the bottom and the part of your hand that you can see is your knuckles, the move is complete when your wrist is on the centreline, from the start to the end of this transition try to imagine you are throwing a ball away to 45 degrees horizontally flush with the ground and off to your right, this may help understand the transition more fully.

Siu Lim Tau (Little Idea)

Tan sau (left side)

Okay so now you know two ways to do tan sau, yep you got it, and here is another way to do it ugh!

From your bong sau position, drop your elbow, which in turn will make you turn your hand, palm faced up and during the transition drop your wrist a couple of inches.

Dai cheung (left side)

By now you should be getting the hang of some of the Chinese terminology, cheung is the word for palm, dai in this instance means downward pointing, so dai cheung means "Downward finger pointing palm strike" okay, so, if you return to the tan sau position and allow your fingers to fall directly away from you so that your fingers are pointing downward and your palm and wrist are facing way from you, thrust your arm directly outward to full extension, pause, and bring your hand horizontal keeping your arm locked out and at full extension, perform heun sau and retract the arm.

Bong sau (right side)

Assuming your stood in yee gee kim yeung ma with your hands at chest height and your elbows are chambered in one smooth action open your right hand and bring your forearm out while turning over

Siu Lim Tau (Little Idea)

your hand so your little finger is on the top and your thumb is on the bottom and the part of your hand that you can see is your knuckles, the move is complete when your wrist is on the centreline.

Tan sau (right side)

From your bong sau position, drop your elbow, which in turn will make you turn your hand, palm faced up and during the transition drop your wrist a couple of inches.

Dai cheung (right side)

Allow your fingers to fall directly away from you so that your fingers are pointing downward and your palm and wrist are facing way from you, thrust your arm directly outward to full extension, pause, and bring your hand horizontal keeping your arm locked out and at full extension, perform heun sau and retract the arm.

Tut sau

Tut sau or toot sau exists for breaking the grip of an aggressor who was able to get a good grip in your wrist.

While in yee gee kim yeung ma with your hands at chest height and your elbows are chambered drop and fully extend your left arm outward at a 45 degree angle, bring the back of your right hand and place it on the forearm of the left arm just below the inside of the elbow.

In one flowing action, slide your right hand down along the forearm; towards the wrist of the left hand while simultaneously bringing up your left wrist to meet your right hand.

Siu Lim Tau (Little Idea)

This action should break the grip of the aggressor, your right hand should travel down to full extension and your left hand should now be rested on the top of the forearm of the right arm.

Again, in one flowing action, slide your left hand down along the forearm; towards the wrist of the right hand while simultaneously bringing up your right wrist to meet your left hand.

This time your left hand should travel down to full extension and your right hand should now be rested on the top of the forearm of the left arm.

One more time in one flowing action, slide your right hand down along the forearm; towards the wrist of the left hand while simultaneously bringing up your left wrist to meet your right hand.

Siu Lim Tau (Little Idea)

Slightly different this time, ready for the next technique, your right hand should travel down to full extension and your left hand takes up the wu sau position and hold it there.

Lin wan kuen

As you can see the Cantonese word for fist in the title you can assume it's got something to do with a punch, so, what is "lin wan", this translates as chain or many or simultaneous, you get the idea, so this is chain punching the last thing that you are taught in the form Siu Lim Tau.

So from your previous position make a fist with the left wu sau hand and launch it directly forward though the centreline to full extension at the same time bring your lower right hand up and make a fist, place the right hand where the left was.

So now you have your left hand fully extended and fist clenched after completing a punch and your right hand is ready to punch.

Keeping your left hand fully extended, drop it just far enough so that the arm leaves the way clear for the other arm to travel through the centreline.

Siu Lim Tau (Little Idea)

Launch the punch with the right hand while at the same time bringing your left hand back and placing it where the right hand started.

So now you have your right hand fully extended and fist clenched after completing a punch, and your left hand ready to punch.

Keeping your right hand fully extended, drop your hand just far enough so that the arm leaves the way clear for the other arm to travel through the centreline.

Launch the punch with left the hand and at the same time bring your right hand back to the chambered position, keep your left arm fully extended, and perform heun sau then chamber the left hand.

Siu Lim Tau (Little Idea)

Fully extend the arm, and then start to bend in the fingers.

Siu Lim Tau (Little Idea)

Continue round to complete huen sau and make a fist.

Siu Lim Tau (Little Idea)

Bring your right foot up and set it next to the left foot

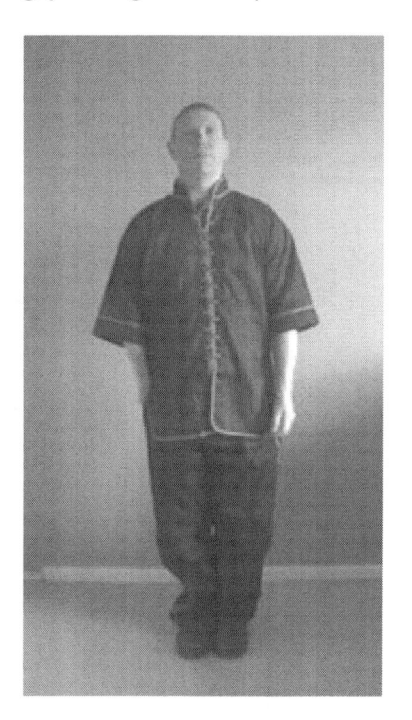

This completes the full Siu Lim Tau, well done, now that you know the full form you should practice it every day to improve it, I personally after getting dressed each morning perform the Siu Lim Tau once, it only takes a few minutes and after a while it becomes part of your daily routine.

Siu Lim Tau (Little Idea)

Chapter 6 - Using the techniques

Punching – (Lin wan kuen)

Chain punching was just explained at the end of the form and is enacted exactly the same way so rather than tell you how to do it again, practice the punching this way.

If I shout 1

Then do one punch

I will count to 10 and on each count do one punch

If I shout out two

Then punch once with whatever hand is at the back and then punch again with the rear hand

I will count on to 10 and on each count do two punches

If I shout out three

Then punch once with whatever hand is at the back and then punch again with the rear hand and then punch again with the rear hand

I will count on to 10 and on each count do three punches

Repeat this exercise right up to six

If I shout out six

Then punch once with whatever hand is at the back and then punch

Siu Lim Tau (Little Idea)

again with the rear hand and then punch again with the rear hand and then punch again with the rear hand and then punch again with the rear hand and then punch again with the rear hand.

I will count on to 10 and on each count do six punches

Turning (Cheun Ma)

From yee gee kim yeung ma, if you turn to the left, note at all times keep looking forward, let your left foot travel through 90 degrees in the direction you move in this case left, your hips should be at 45 degrees and both of your feet should be at 45 degrees and parallel to each other, to recap waist and feet at 45 degrees to your left. Your rear leg should be supporting you, and, have the balance, your front leg should have no weight on it at all the weight ratio on your legs is 100% / 0%.

The next step is to turn to your right 90 degrees, this is tricky at first, and note that both of your feet should remain on the ground, DO NOT turn on the balls of your feet and DO NOT turn on the heels of your feet, the whole foot must be on the ground when you turn and BOTH FEET turn at the same time.

There should always be a pause for a second or two and then do the same thing to return to the left 90 degrees.

Tip: while in this stance to prove that there is no weight on the back leg, lift your front leg and try to notice if you had to re-adjust your body position so that the balance was properly on the back leg thus allowing you to lift the front leg. Check this periodically and always take your time to get things right.

Siu Lim Tau (Little Idea)

Turning Punch

Now using the turning you have been practicing above start including the Wing Chun punch, when you have completed the turn, note which leg has a 100% of the weight on it and punch through the centreline on that side... pause... do the turn... and then repeat it on the other side. (The punch should land at the same time as the turn completes. The aim is to use the turn to add power to the punch amongst other things) Again do these for at least a minimum of 10 times on each side.

Tip: when you here the word dar or da on the end of a technique it refers to both hands being used at the same time (simultaneous attack and defence)

Stepping (Biu Ma)

Just like cheun ma and from yee gee kim yeung ma, if you turn to the left, first turn your head to the left to look in the direction you are going then let your left foot travels through 90 degrees in the direction you move i.e. left, your hips should be at 45 degrees and both of your feet should be at 45 degrees and parallel to each other all of this, in the direction you are facing, to recap waist and feet at 45 degrees to your left. Your rear leg should be supporting you, and, have the balance, your front leg should have no weight on it at all, the weight ratio on your legs is 100% / 0%.

You are now ready to make your first Wing Chun Step, sink a little bit on your weight bearing leg so that you do not fall forward exposing your chin to an opponents fist, at the same time lift your front leg and push yourself off the ball and toes of your weight bearing leg thus launching yourself forward, when you land, land on the ball of the front foot and sit back down in your stance so that all

Siu Lim Tau (Little Idea)

the weight returns to the weight bearing leg and there is nothing on the front leg.

Siu Lim Tau (Little Idea)

Gum sau bear hug escape

While in a bear hug from behind you, bend your knees and push your hand backwards this will release the grip allowing you to continue the attack.

Setting up bong sau

Bong sau can be confusing to start off with for the beginner as its use is not always apparent, people try to use it to deflect on coming force which is wrong, bong sau translated as wing arm is meant for making contact, once contact has been made, switch to a more effect technique/concept to take control of the fight.

To set up bong sau put your left arm out in front of you and fully extended it parallel to your shoulder, from your elbow allow your forearm and hand to drop across your centre, you are now in bong

Siu Lim Tau (Little Idea)

sau, to test if your bong sau is in the right place, hold your wrist with your right hand and drop your left elbow, your left arm should now be in tan sau, check to see if there is a one fist distance between your left elbow and torso if there is not, then slightly adjust your elbow position accordingly and make sure your tan sau is on the centreline, hold on to your left wrist with your right hand again, and raise your elbow to shoulder height, if you followed my instructions correctly, then you should be in a good bong sau, note the position and always test bong sau using the method I have explained here.

Jum sau

Protect the centre line   Strike through

Siu Lim Tau (Little Idea)

Long bridge up and down

Siu Lim Tau (Little Idea)

Don chi sau

Don chi sau translates as single sticking hand; we don't spend a lot of time at the single sticking hand but long enough time for you to get the feel for things to come, without the confusion of two hands and your brain having to understand too many messages in one fell swoop. You do need a partner to train this properly so that you can start to respond too the messages your partners arm is giving you, but you can practice each side separately in the air, practicing each side in the air with no pressure I find, is a good way to start training this because when two newish students come together it becomes clash of force where each student adds more pressure as the other does to compensate which is wrong, the touch, between the two chi sau partners should be very light with the each persons arm aiming for the partners centreline.

| tan sau | ching cheung | bong sau |

Don chi sau as partner 1

Take up your yee gee kim yeung ma stance and have your arms withdrawn, bring your left arm forward and position it in tan

Siu Lim Tau (Little Idea)

sau, pause, then switch to ching cheung, only moving forward a couple of inches, again pause, then switch to bong sau, again pause and return to tan sau where you started and repeat the drill over and over again till you become proficient.

| fook sau | jut sau | punch |

Don chi sau as partner 2

This side starts off in fook sau, so take up your yee gee kim yeung ma stance and have your arms withdrawn, bring your left arm forward and position it in the fook sau position and after a small pause change to jut sau, again make a small pause and launch a punch but only moving forward approximately two inches, return to fook sau once again and repeat over and over again until you can do it well.

Siu Lim Tau (Little Idea)

Ching sun gerk

There are no kicks in the Siu Lim Tau form, so the first time you see kicks properly is in the next form which is Chum Kiu, with that said we always introduce the student to the front kick at the introduction of the first form, so translating ching sun gerk, by now you have heard the word ching or jing meaning forward or front, the other key word here is the gerk, gerk translates as foot giving us a rough translation of front kick, in Wing Chun we don't snap kicks, so while standing in a lead leg stance lift your lead legs knee directly up, let your toes drop pointing to the ground, whip up your toes as if somebody has got hold of your toes, kick out and to waist height, note that the point of contact should be the heal of the foot. if you find yourself off balance then bend the knee of the weight bearing leg, thus dropping your centre of gravity even further and improving your balance, it will take a while to build the leg strength of the weight bearing leg so keep practicing it and you will get stronger and better at the kick.

Siu Lim Tau (Little Idea)

Chapter 7 – The full Siu Lim Tau

Siu Lim Tau - Section 1

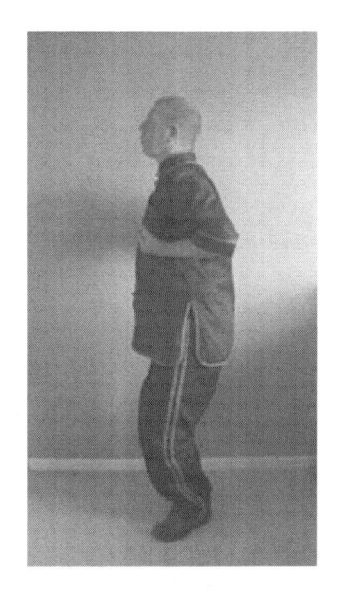

Siu Lim Tau (Little Idea)

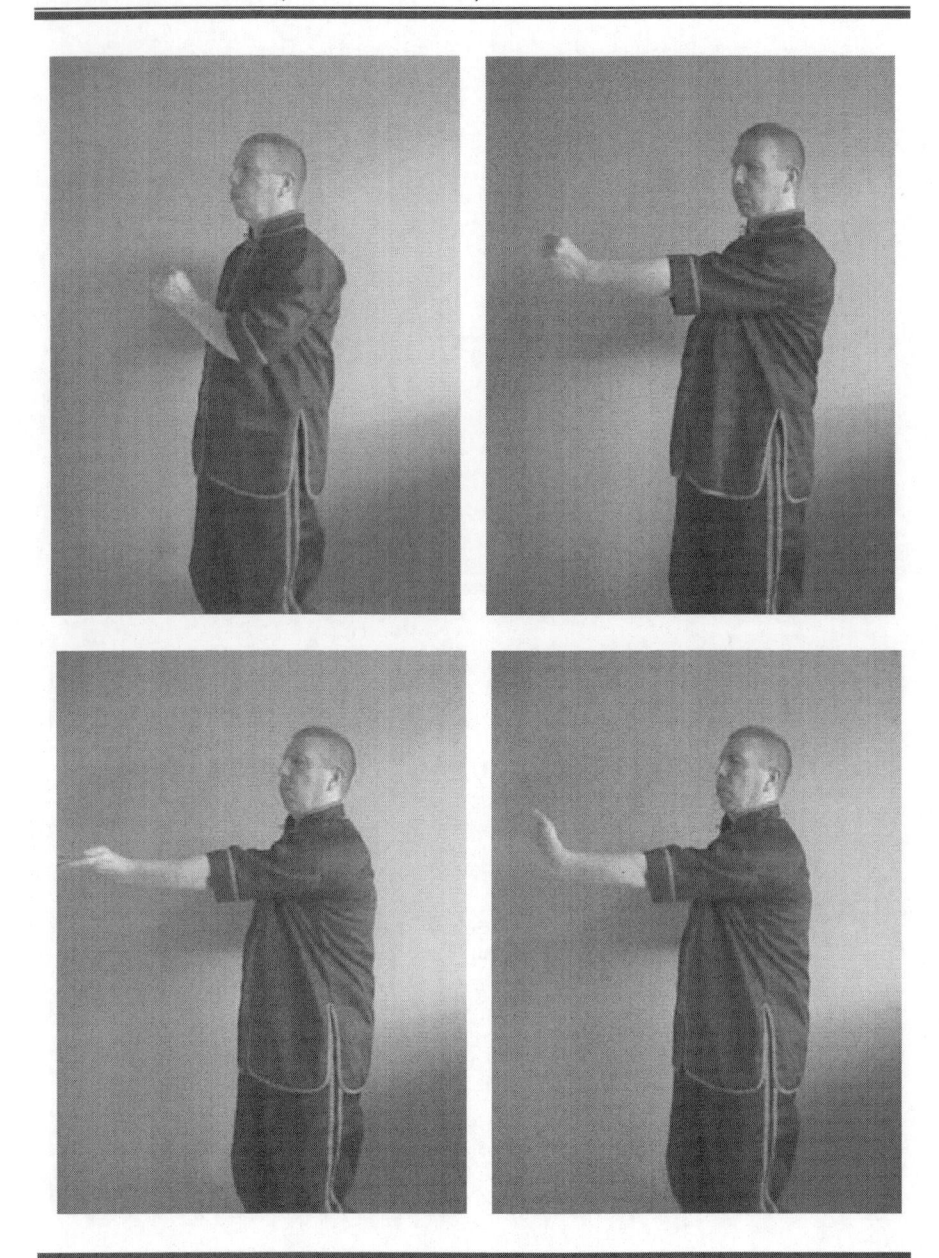

Siu Lim Tau (Little Idea)

Siu Lim Tau (Little Idea)

Repeat on the right hand side

Siu Lim Tau (Little Idea)

Siu Lim Tau (Little Idea)

Siu Lim Tau (Little Idea)

Repeat pages 79 to 80 three times

Siu Lim Tau (Little Idea)

Siu Lim Tau (Little Idea)

Repeat everything from page 79 to here on the right hand side.

Siu Lim Tau (Little Idea)

Siu Lim Tau - Section 2

Siu Lim Tau (Little Idea)

Siu Lim Tau (Little Idea)

Siu Lim Tau (Little Idea)

Siu Lim Tau (Little Idea)

Siu Lim Tau (Little Idea)

Siu Lim Tau (Little Idea)

Siu Lim Tau (Little Idea)

Siu Lim Tau - Section 3

Siu Lim Tau (Little Idea)

Siu Lim Tau (Little Idea)

Repeat on the right hand side

Siu Lim Tau (Little Idea)

Siu Lim Tau (Little Idea)

Siu Lim Tau (Little Idea)

Siu Lim Tau (Little Idea)

Repeat on the right hand side

Siu Lim Tau (Little Idea)

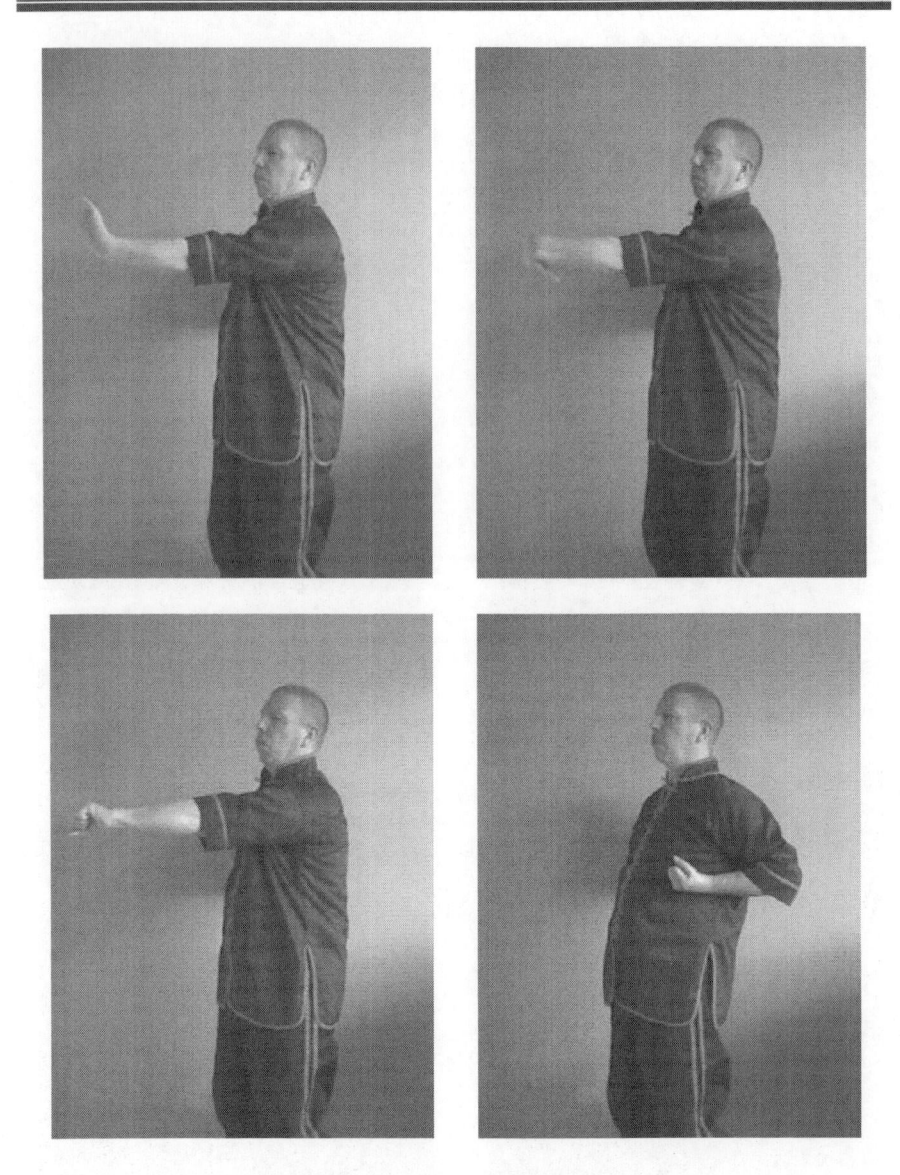

Siu Lim Tau (Little Idea)

Repeat on the right hand side

Siu Lim Tau (Little Idea)

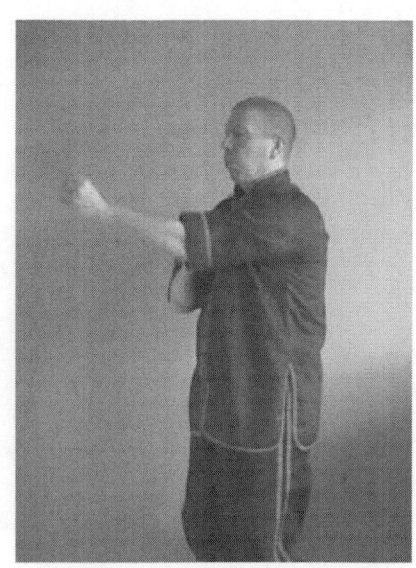

Siu Lim Tau (Little Idea)

Siu Lim Tau (Little Idea)

Siu Lim Tau (Little Idea)

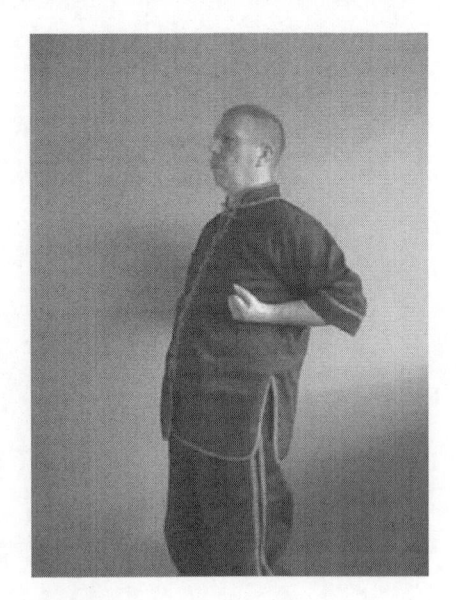

The end of the form

Printed in Great Britain by
Amazon.co.uk, Ltd.,
Marston Gate.